SCHIRMER'S LIBRARY
OF MUSICAL CLASSICS

T0058861

OTTAKAR ŠEVČÍK

Op. 2

The School of Bowing Technic

Escuela de la Técnica del Arco

Systematically and Progressively
Graded Bowing Exercises for the Violin

Preparatory exercises. Rhythmic exercises and dividing
of the bow-length. Detached and hopping styles of
bowing. Exercise in sustained tones and in economizing
the bow-length, i. e., holding it back as much as possible.

English Translations by
DR. THEODORE BAKER

Traducción española de
S. LOPEZ MIRANDA

Part I | Part II
Library Vol. 1182 | → Library Vol. 1183

Edited and Fingered by
PHILIPP MITTELL

G. SCHIRMER, Inc.

DISTRIBUTED BY
HAL•LEONARD®
CORPORATION
7777 W. BLUEMOUND RD. P.O. BOX 13819 MILWAUKEE, WI 53213

Part II

No. 13

Study in Triplets
With 105 Variants in the Bowing

For the same Study in the 7th position, see No. 26.

Parte II

Nº 13

Estudio en Tresillos
con 105 cambios de golpes de arco

El mismo en la 7ª posición, véase Nº 26.

4

Bowings
Golpes de Arco

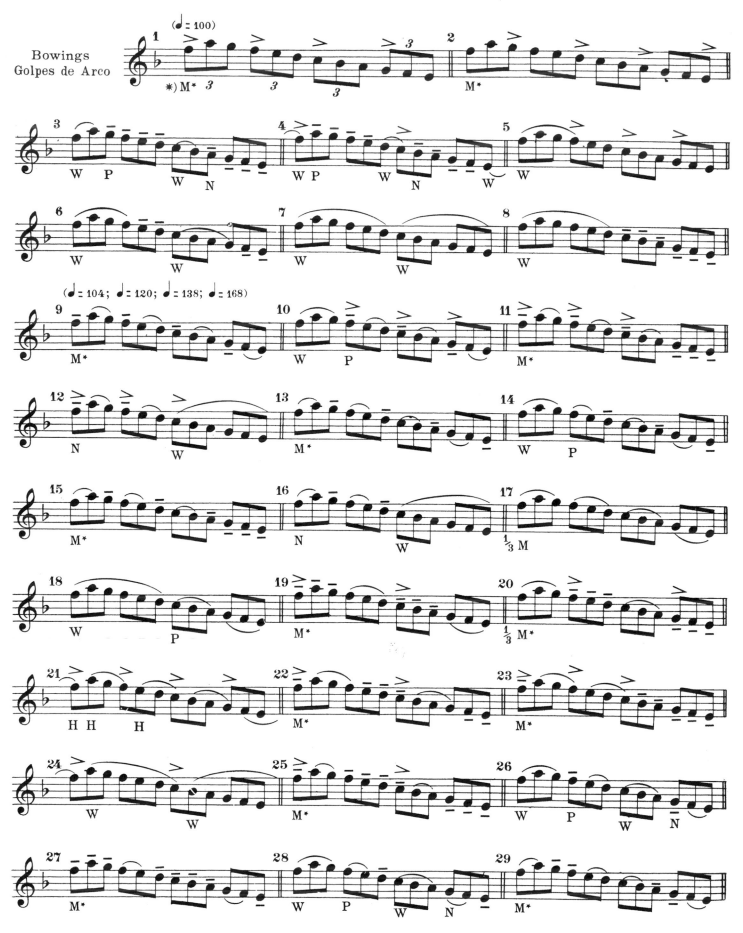

No.14

Study in Triplets (three-four time) with 77 different Bowings

For the same Study in the 4th position, see No.25.

Nº 14

Estudios en Tresillos (compás $\frac{3}{4}$) con 77 cambios de golpes de arco

El mismo estudio en la 4ª posición, véase Nº 25.

No. 15

Study in Sixteenth-Notes
(six-eight time)
with 64 different Bowings

For the same Study in the 4th position, see No. 27.

Nº 15

Estudio en semicorcheas
(compás $\frac{6}{8}$)
con 64 cambios de golpes de arco

El mismo estudio en la 4ª posición, véase Nº 27.

Allegro moderato

Bowings
Golpes de Arco

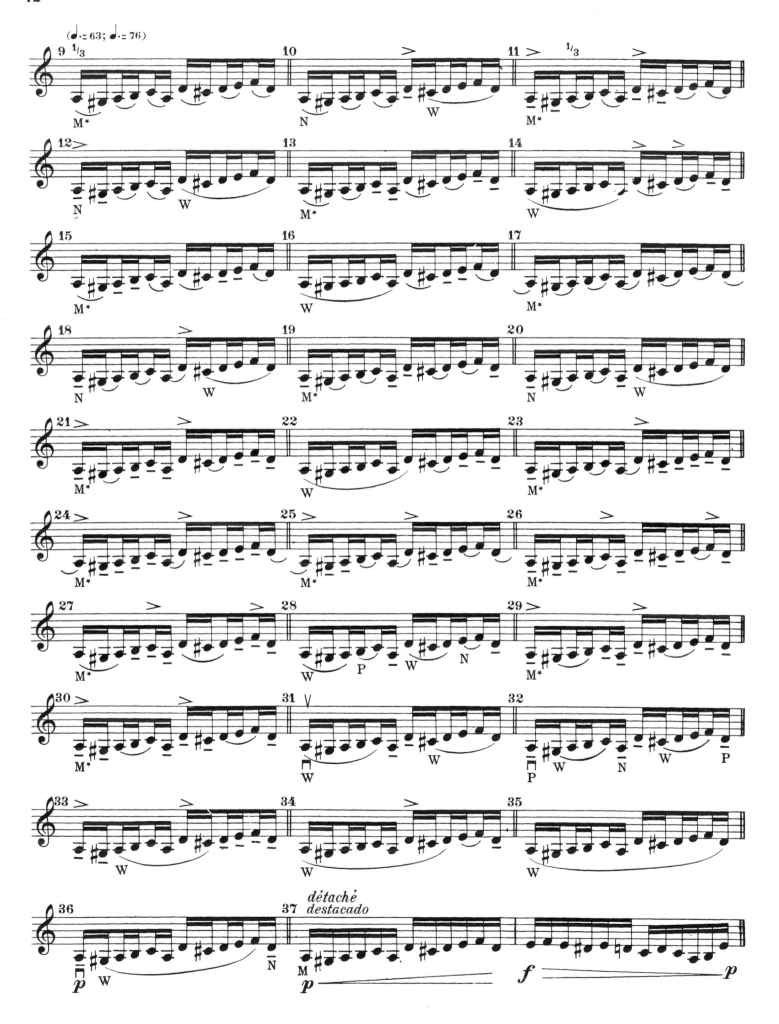

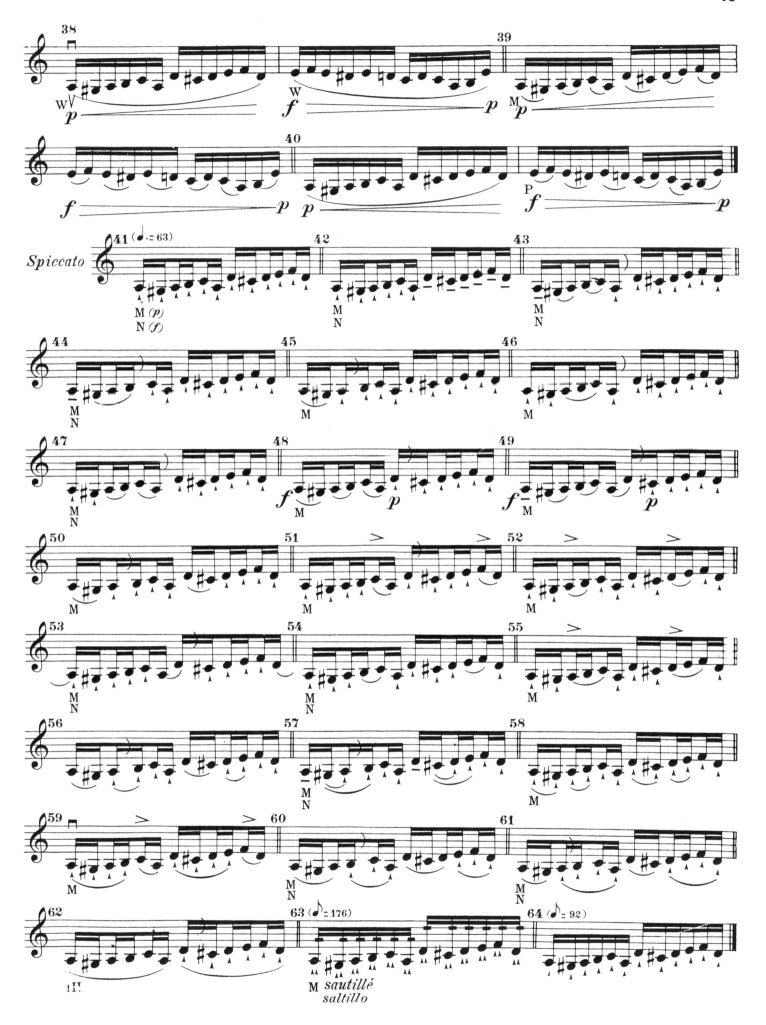

No. 16

Study in Sixteenth-Notes
(three-four time)
with 68 different Bowings

Nº 16

Estudio en semicorcheas
(compás $\frac{3}{4}$)
con 68 cambios de golpes de arco

No. 17

Study in Sixteenth-Notes
(four-four, or common, time)
with 131 different Bowings

For the same Study in the 5th position, see No. 28.

Nº 17

Estudio en semicorcheas
(compás 4/4 ó Compasillo)
con 131 cambios de golpes de arco

El mismo estudio en la 5ª posición, véase Nº 28

18

*) The second half of each measure exactly like the first. | *) La segunda mitad del compás, como la primera.

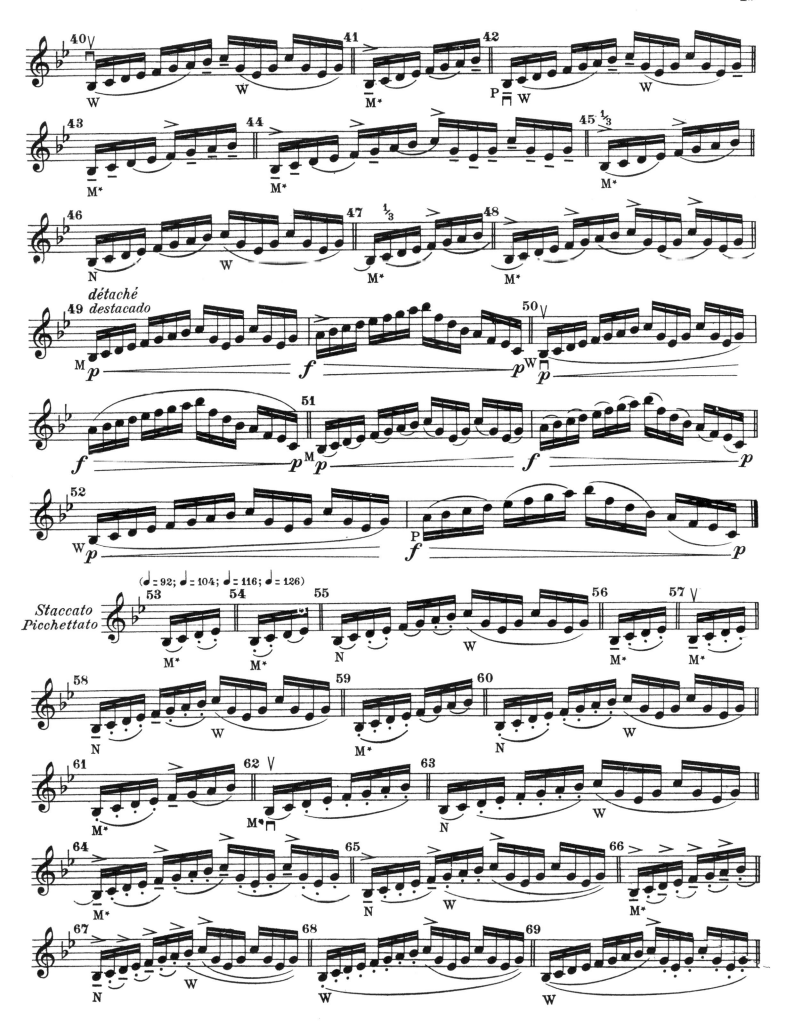

19

Dotted Sixteenths
Semicorcheas
con puntillo

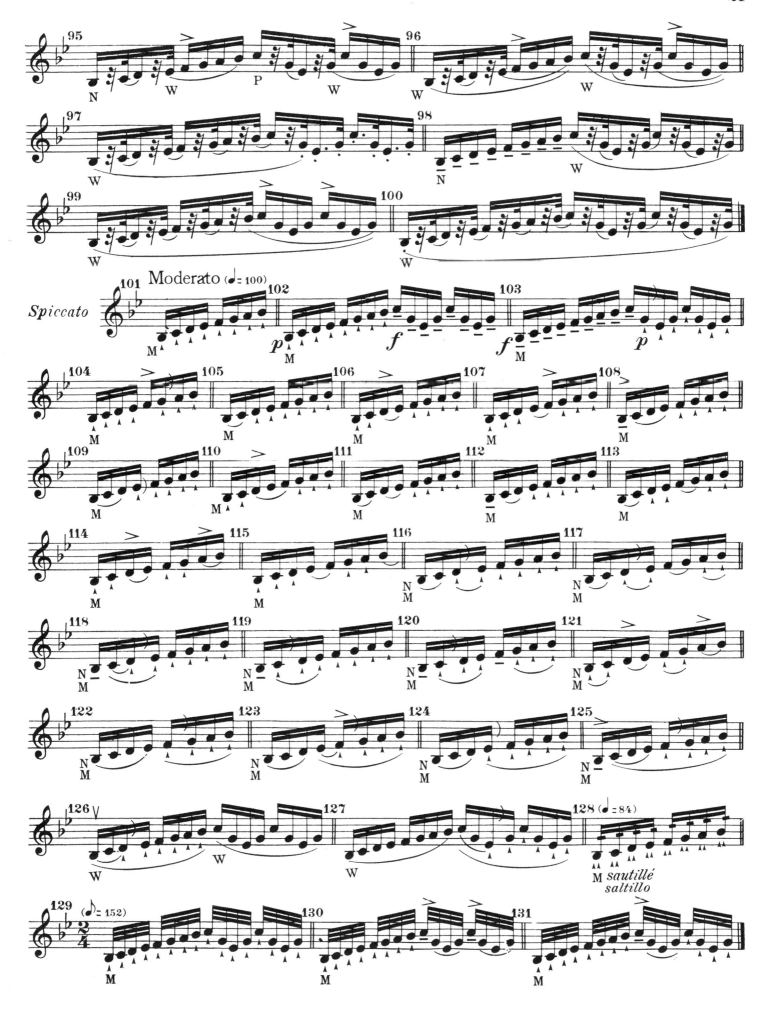

22

Pianissimo Exercises
over the Fingerboard
For Developing Softness of Tone

Ejercicios en *pp (pianissimo)*
sobre el Diapasón (ó Batidor)
para obtener la dulzura en el sonido

No. 18

Exercise with 30 Variants

Nº 18

Ejemplo con 30 Variaciones

Variants | Variaciones

No. 19

Pianissimo Exercises
over the Fingerboard
(continued)

Exercise with 59 Variants

Nº 19

Continuación de los Ejercicios
en *pp* *(pianissimo)*
sobre el Diapasón (ó Batidor)

Estudio con 59 Variaciones

No. 20

Exercise
on Sustained Tones
for economizing the bow

Practise preceding Studies 3 to 7, and 13 to 17, in the following ways:

a) In groups of two measures to one bow f
b) In groups of four measures to one bow p
c) In groups of eight measures to one bow ppp

All pages referred to below are in Book I, except for exercise 14.

Nº 20

Ejercicio en notas largas (sostenidas)
y de la retención del Arco, ejemp.
sosteniéndole de talón á punta
y vice-versa todo lo más posible

Practíquense los estudios precedentes Nº 3 á 7 y 13 a 17 en las formas siguientes:

a) en grupos de 2 compases en una sola arcada f
b) en grupos de 4 compases en una sola arcada p
c) en grupos de 8 compases en una sola arcada ppp

Las páginas á que más abajo nos referimos están todas en el Libro Iº, con excepción del ejercicio No. 14.

Allegro

No.14.

etc.

page 8
página 8

Exercises in Arpeggios
(Broken Chords)
across 3 and 4 strings,
using the preceding styles of bowing

No. 21

With Bowings 1 to 97
in No.13

Ejercicios en acordes arpegiados
sobre tres y cuatro cuerdas,
aplicándoseles los golpes
de arco precedentes

Nº 21

Con los golpes de arco
indicados en los Nᵒˢ1 á 97 del Nº13

No. 22

With the Bowings Given in No.16

Nº 22

Con los golpes de arco del Nº 16

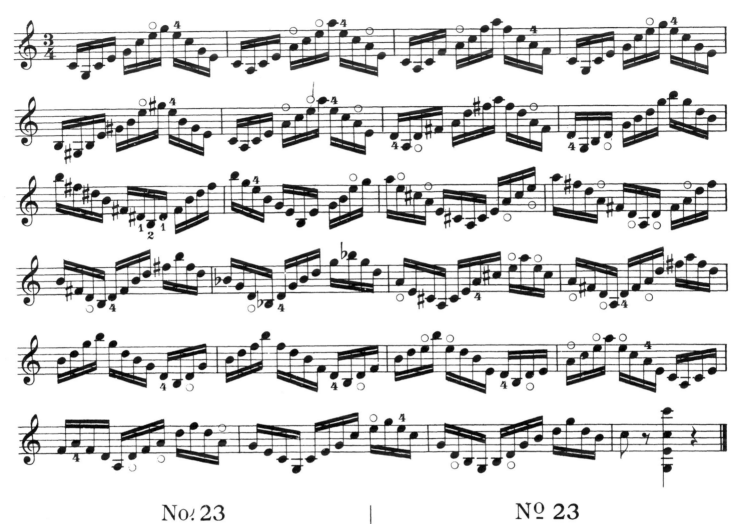

No. 23

With the Bowings Given in No.17

Nº 23

Con los golpes de arco del Nº 17

No. 24

With the Bowings Given in No.15

Nº 24

Con los golpes de arco del Nº 15

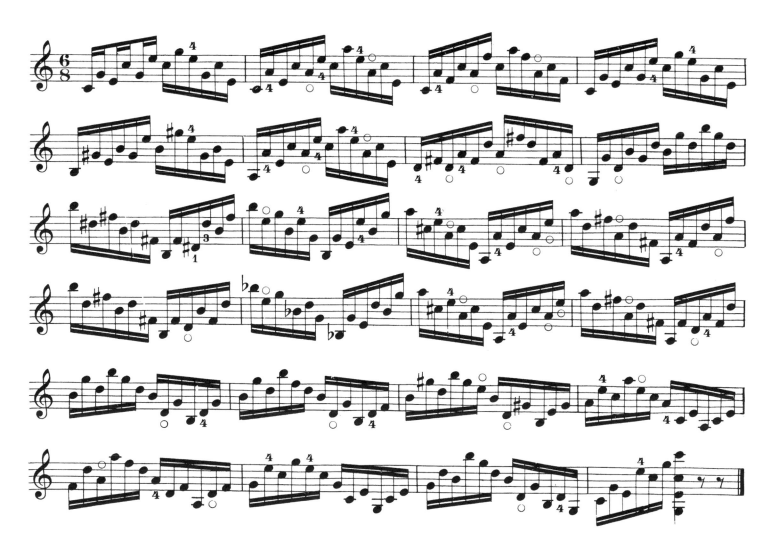

Employment of the Preceding Bowings
in the High Positions

Empleo de los golpes de arco precedentes
en las posiciones superiores

No. 25

Nº 25

With the Bowings Given in No. 14

Con los golpes de arco del Nº 14

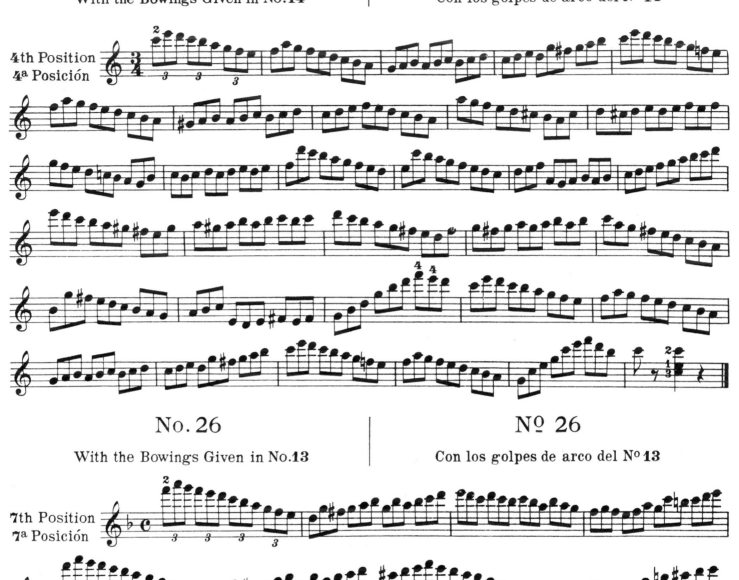

4th Position
4ª Posición

No. 26

Nº 26

With the Bowings Given in No. 13

Con los golpes de arco del Nº 13

7th Position
7ª Posición

No. 27

With the Bowings Given in No. 15

N⁰ 27

Con los golpes de arco del N⁰ 15

4th Position
5ª Posición

No. 28

With the Bowings Given in No. 17

N⁰ 28

Con los golpes de arco del N⁰ 17

4th Position
4ª Posición